The Story of Scary Bear and the Pumpkin Patch

Co-Authors
TC LiFonti
Charles "Peanut" Tillman

Illustrator
Gabrielle Esposito

Charles Tillman

CORNERSTONE
33
FOUNDATION

All book titles benefit the Charles Tillman Cornerstone Foundation.

ISBN-13: 978-0692286081
ISBN-10: 069228608X

An additional special thanks to Karen Hahn and Paul Faris.

With Halloween only three days away,
Scary Bear waited anxiously for Papa Bear
to come home so they could go pick out
their pumpkins.

"Mama Bear, Mama Bear!" Scary Bear said. "When are we going to the pumpkin patch to get our pumpkins?"

Mama Bear smiled, "Be patient, Scary Bear, honey. Papa Bear is on his way home. He will be here shortly."

Dressed and ready to leave, Scary Bear
sat on the stairs and watched the door.
And as he waited, and waited, and waited,
he grew more and more sleepy...

"...I am home," Papa Bear said as he walked through the door. "Are you ready to go pick out a pumpkin?"

Scary Bear jumped up, "Yes! Yes, I am! Let's go! I've been so good. Let's go, Papa Bear!"

As soon as they arrived, Scary Bear raced directly into the pumpkin patch.

"Scary Bear, buddy," Papa Bear warned.
"Do not go too far.
Stay close to me so you don't..."

...but Scary Bear wasn't listening.
He was already into the field of pumpkins
looking for the biggest one he could find.

Then, after a moment, he looked around and saw that he was all alone. The sky was slowly dimming darker, and the green grasses were gradually growing taller.

For the first time, Scary Bear
was worried. He had traveled too far
away from Papa Bear
and he didn't know what to do.

"Papa Bear! Papa Bear!"
Scary Bear called over and over...

...but there was no answer.
He wished he had not run off so quickly.

"Papa Bear!" he shouted one more time...

...but he was all alone.

Scary Bear started turning in all different directions—he was so confused.

And everywhere he looked, the tall, dark stalks made it difficult to see anything clearly.

He was afraid that he would never find his way back.

All of a sudden, Scary Bear heard a noise and he wanted to see if it was Papa Bear...

...so he peeked through the green grasses,
and looked over the plump pumpkins,
and what he found was...

...a Scary Scarecrow pointing down at him.

"Scary Bear," the Scary Scarecrow laughed.
"Now you are lost. You should have
stayed close to Papa Bear."

When Scary Bear heard the Scary Scarecrow's voice, he turned and ran.

But, while running, his foot became tangled in a vine and he fell to the ground. He believed the Scary Scarecrow was getting closer to him.

Quickly, Scary Bear closed his eyes and sniffled, "I wish Papa Bear was here."

Suddenly, as he was being lifted up, he covered his eyes with his paws and felt...

...he was being cradled and hugged.
He opened his eyes to find
Papa Bear holding him.

"You were sleeping
on the staircase,
buddy,"
Papa Bear said.
"It was all just
a bad dream.
Everything's okay."

And Scary Bear
gave Papa Bear
a big bear hug
and smiled.

When they arrived at the real pumpkin patch, they both laughed as Scary Bear told Papa Bear about his bad dream.

As soon as they returned home, they started to carve their pumpkins together.

And when they were finished,
they set up their pumpkins and were now
ready for Halloween.

The End.

SONYA MARTIN PHOTOGRAPHY

The mission of the Charles Tillman Cornerstone Foundation is to provide opportunities and resources to children and their families who are in need.

·   ·   ·

A percentage of each book sold will directly benefit the foundation and its efforts to continually help those needing assistance.

Charles Tillman

CORNERSTONE
33
FOUNDATION

www.charlestillman.org

Charles Locker · This program enriches the lives of chronically and critically ill children by providing them and their families with access to iPads, notebook computers, DVD players, portable Play Station game systems, and other electronic handheld games, to pass the time during recovery and treatment.

Field of Dreams · A program that provides chronically and critically ill children and their families with magical memories by fulfilling sports-related wishes. Throughout the year, we offer unique opportunities including tickets to Bears games.

Holiday Celebration · In December, Charles, his wife, Jackie, and a few of Santa's elves visit Chicago-area hospitals to pass out gifts, visit with families and partake in hospital activities, like bingo, to help spread holiday cheer.

TendHER Heart Luncheon · Each spring more than 150 mothers of critically and chronically ill children are invited to attend a special brunch, honoring them for the sacrifices they make in caring for their ill child. The brunch will provide these women with the opportunity to "take a minute" for themselves and enjoy each other's company and support.

Tiana Fund · The Tiana Fund program provides assistance to economically at-risk persons or families in-need that will strengthen their ability to care for themselves, enhance their stability and security, and improve their quality of life or their ability to contribute to the community. Applications are only available at Chicago-area hospitals or pre-approved community organizations.

41378310R00025